CONJURING AN EPIPHANY

poems by

Deborah Purdy

Finishing Line Press
Georgetown, Kentucky

CONJURING AN EPIPHANY

Copyright © 2022 by Deborah Purdy
ISBN 978-1-64662-725-7 First Edition
All rights reserved under International and Pan-American Copyright Conventions. No part of this book may be reproduced in any manner whatsoever without written permission from the publisher, except in the case of brief quotations embodied in critical articles and reviews.

ACKNOWLEDGMENTS

American Poetry Journal: "Good Lines for a Fortunate Life"
Aurorean: "New Year's Eve"
Black Bough Poetry: "Full Moon"
Blue Nib: "I Predict"
Cleaver Magazine: "Lab Child Theorem"
Door Is A Jar: "Pictures on the Piano"
Gingerbread House: "Wild Onions"
Heat the Grease Anthology: "My Grandmother's Kitchen Fifty Years Later"
Nail Polish Stories: "Master Plan"

Publisher: Leah Huete de Maines
Editor: Christen Kincaid
Cover Art: Deborah Purdy
Author Photo: Deborah Purdy
Cover Design: Elizabeth Maines McCleavy

Order online: www.finishinglinepress.com
also available on amazon.com

Author inquiries and mail orders:
Finishing Line Press
PO Box 1626
Georgetown, Kentucky 40324
USA

Table of Contents

Barn Swallows 1
Once Upon a Time 2
In the Time of Home 3
I Predict 4
Nocturnal Ritual 5
Three Things 6
Night School 7
A Long Year 8
Opening the Box 9
Good Lines for a Fortunate Life 10
Will Work for Letters 11
Persephone's Side of the Story 12
Moon 13
Free Fall 14
New Year's Eve 15
Milkweed 16
Late Autumn in the Mountains 17
Pictures on the Piano 18
Mistaken Identity 19
Lab Child Theorem 20
Looking 21
Full Moon 22
The Waving Girl in Savannah 23
Empty Houses 24
Offerings 25
Natural Habits 26
Family Curse 27
My Grandmother's Kitchen Fifty Years Later 28
Hardwired 29
Disconnection 30
Master Plan 31
Spelling It Out 32
In the Cards 33
Change of Plans 34
Wild Onions 35
Written in the Stars 36

Barn Swallows

Mine are not the only ghosts here.
We survey stone and beam, try to
redeem time by putting it
in its place.

We're startled by passerine wings
cobalt-backed with a flash
of cinnamon, a metallic glide and rise
in concert on the current outside.

Our sky has been revised, our river
reconfigured to accommodate the reluctance
of a reclusive muse. Does it all
come down to the tenure of fire,

that elastic tunnel of grace and flight?
We look for light in the myth of pleasing
but we can't step back
or even stand still.

Once Upon a Time

In 1969 we found the moon and the music.
We knew the names of stars and listened

to their words in our dreams and in our cars.
Discordant smoke signals snarled our traffic.

The finish line was close enough to contradict us.
It was possible to have blind faith and a suspicious mind.

The world was never kind but there were options.
A net transpired to put the unfamiliar in place.

In the Time of Home

Evening invites shadows of questions
you didn't know you had.

You have to pick and choose
among the ghosts allowed to haunt you.

This home in your bones,
this time of a place

soothes over the scars of days
of sweet tea and insincerity—

You have to let the past float away
like a river on its way home.

I Predict
> *after Lorine Niedecker*

you will change your mind
with words
        you do not know.
        If you choose—
knowing.

I read the book
long out of fashion.
        You once said
        it was easy, wed

to writing.

A labyrinth
lodges no link—
        Behind
        we find
knowledge

comfort.
We praise
        the secrets
        among syllables.
We speak—

Nocturnal Ritual

In the middle of the night
it's the edge of time—

A dusky world of threads
and drums, threats and glitches.

A solitary subject
under a spell—

Conclusions and delusions
unraveling like wild vines.

Three Things

Three strikes and you're out
but the third time's the charm—

If you're lucky
you'll be granted three wishes

and the three wise women
will be on your side, wayward

even as they weave
the triangle of your life.

Night School

Gliding by like the smoke of visions
it evens out over the vacant school
spreading over it like a long black coat.

In the harbored night a scarf of stars
settles across the sky, offering lessons
like blessings from a portal to a world

you've never known, a world
not here but where it wants to be.
The wind argues back and forth with itself.

A Long Year

You won't miss your voice—
It stays in the body, it stays in the mind

and resurrects your name
in the brushstrokes of shadows.

We fall from the sum of stories
spelled in paper clips and sips of coffee,

a figment of a small world under a sky
away from winter. We waste

our monopoly money with the curve
of a word—and have nothing to show for it.

Opening the Box

It was probably a jar
Or a can of worms

The price of fire
A trick, a miscalculation

All the great sorrows
Distresses and disappointments

Complications and curses
Evil and grief

No remedy, no cure
Unless you count hope

Good Lines for a Fortunate Life
    after "Lines for the Fortunate Cookies" by Frank O'Hara

Just when you think you have arrived, the time changes.
I wonder if you know what you are thinking.

You will meet a stranger at Starbucks and exchange names.
You will travel to Paris and have breakfast at McDonald's.

You will marry the first person you meet who has a sister.
The next person you dream about will try to take advantage of you.

That's not a hat on your head, it's your brain leaking.
At times, strangers may wonder what you are thinking.

Your first novel will be adapted for television.
If you write a poem, it will be famous.

Please check your messages for a reminder from the library.
Steven Spielberg is looking for you.

Drink some tea to relieve your conscience.
You may wonder what it means but others will understand.

I realize you drive an SUV, but that doesn't mean you'll live FOREVER!
Most people wish they could meet you.

You are a prisoner in a zoo and don't know which animal you are.
What makes you think this is true?

In the end YOU will decide what you are thinking.
Now that you've arrived, where are you going?

Will Work for Letters

I need a word
to take the blame,

share the costs
of our mutual seclusion.

I need a vowel
if Vanna could loan

it—one that rhymes
at the end of the day.

I need a ticket for
a magic carpet ride—

that invisible
unaffordable excursion.

Persephone's Side of the Story

Everyone says it was my fault
but that was another legend.

Whisked from my mother's
meadow, from flowers to fire

into the depths of someone
else's ruling, deceived

by a seed I didn't recognize.
None of it was my idea.

I never wanted to be Queen
in the realm of the Dead

where no one is allowed
to speak my name

but I know no spells
to change the story.

Moon

In the center of the moon the ice is melting
into the shine of the streetlight's glare.

The stare of the moon into starlight
straddles the cracks in the center of night.

The streetlight blinks and evening curves
into morning, the moon delirious, disappearing.

Free Fall

Under the spell of the circle of time
there's no straight line to certainty.

In the spirit of bad weather
we summon the storm,

dance on thin ice,
skate on the sand.

It's the luck of the dawn—
We fall in and out of place.

New Year's Eve

One year is folding up
Into the accordion

Of those that came before—
A soup stew of to do and not yet done.

The next remains unraveled
Yet to be revealed

Moon by moon, word
By word, both spoken

And silent, frozen
In the evening air.

Milkweed

Wayside wildweed seeded
windblown pod—

Pick it and you can split the stalk,
string or spill

mythical consolations and corruptions,
sweetener, sap, sustenance.

Stretch the milk—
A drop could seal your fingers

or poison on an arrow.
You might be tempted to sip

but make sure you don't swallow.

Late Autumn in the Mountains

Canadian geese in timeless formation
unfurl in a curling ribbon above us,

Spare branches beckon
to a moonstone sky,

Hollow and lingering
like sorrow in the stillness.

Pictures on the Piano

In a corner of the room
In a corner of a life
The piano fills the space
Of hours now turned

Into ashes. Photographs
On the piano remain
The same, but one sister
Gets older

And the other never ages
Among the dust
And the frames
And the silence.

Mistaken Identity

I'm no magician—
It's an old family curse

like music ringing
in your ears and running

down your wrist.
I make no predictions—

It's a journey in a thimble
from a timetable in a pocket.

Lab Child Theorem

Automatic habit
like a rifle, pistol
or pilot, the
beach doll hermit
told him to hold
the bracelet, the
bracelet told him
to blame the rich hotel,
the cloth heir,
the rambling hot chili.
He touched the
bridal cloth hem
and breathed in the
child moll—
the label torched him
label child mother
blame cloth hider
blame child other
beamed torched hill.

Looking

When I'm in the bookstore, I look
for Calliope nested on her velvet
throne and wait for her to purr
her permission. She nuzzles my
hand as I stroke her fur and take
a moment before perusing
the bookshelves. I'm not looking
for anything in particular as I'm drawn
to the items on display.
I look through a history of omens
and notice a new deck of oracles.
I handle the crystals as delicate
messengers, roll a selenite wand along
my palm, select a piece
of amethyst in the shape of
a pyramid. I examine a smoky quartz
point. Everything points to the questioning:
cards and marks and manuals for visions
beyond the ordinary. I consider a black
tourmaline pendant on a chain that swings
from a bookend. I thumb through
pages and palm a paperweight
as if it's a crystal ball. Then I pick
up a kaleidoscope and look
into it, imagining
what is impossible
to see.

Full Moon

A feather, a bone
in the shape of a star

suspended from the moon's
last mooring

The shadow of a crow
follows dusk to midnight—

A blur in the wolf's dreaming.

The Waving Girl in Savannah

Florence, now that you live forever
fastened in bronze as legend and everyday life,
some like to stir the stories.

Some like to say
for love, for money, for company.
But maybe it was simply kindness.

Handkerchief, dishtowel or handy kitchen cloth,
sometimes a Sunday scarf,
always a lantern at night.

At night
some say
they still see you,

your dress fluttering
like fireflies in the dark
in the questions that surround you.

Empty Houses

The son marries
and moves into a new life
in the woods among trees
and tall tales of possibilities.

The father shovels snow
one last time, one last
heart beat away
from the time being.

The mother is moved
away, tucked
safely into a new home
in a new city

where nobody visits.
Does the house sigh,
shudder to itself,
as it surrenders

one shingle after another
one shutter after another
one life after another?
The house stands alone —

solemn as a lost soldier
in an army of weeds,
peeling paint, and
vacant-eyed windows

to ancient history
like my grandmother's house
and the Sunday dinners
we used to have there.

Offerings

I can't offer directions
to the path of least resistance

or a story for the altar
in the yard of spare words—

But I can make peace offerings
in the temple of misunderstandings

and send blessings
to stray cats and crows

in the backyard
of my mission.

Natural Habits

Steal a base and chase the music—
The money will find itself in the moonlight
and the world will fight for its finery.
Home is a lock either for or against you.
There may be a reason
in the clear and fierce rumble—
Gift-wrapped in real time,
a swerve on the vulnerable road.
You'll know who you are
when you dodge it—
And losing feels like second nature.

Family Curse

It journeys through pages
on wings of a phoenix.

Who can say where it started—
This brand of bad luck

braided among a line of wives
back to back and into the future.

What strike of a match
ignited this trick of time travel?

Who held good luck in both hands
and tossed it out with the bath water?

It must have been more than
stomping on a crack

or ducking under a ladder.
What strand of spell is this—

Family curse as the course
with no options.

My Grandmother's Kitchen Fifty Years Later

A room dimmed by
distant issues diced and wrecked—
Revealed in recipes
buried in the ashes of memory.

What I remember is this:
oilcloth tossed over the kitchen table,
language in my aunts' assurances,
chopping, stirring, the arrangement

of fried chicken on a platter.
Afterwards
washing dishes with spring water
warmed in the wood stove.

Now the remains are a flavor
flat out and final
welcomings, unwelcomings
wired to what I can no longer taste.

Hardwired

This is the world
we have to live in—

Mr. Rogers doesn't live
next door and we've forgotten

how to break bread.
We make excuses

for chaos and concrete
but choose them anyway

over leaves and grass.
We're hardwired for order

and seek explanations. All patterns
must be present and accounted for.

We look for assurances
in the solace of beauty

but the bad reputation
of familiarity precedes us.

Disconnection

What trickery is this—
Misinformation and malfunctioning motions,

Calling cards left
on the bureau of lost associations.

Withdrawal symptoms from an alien point of view—
Chances are the puzzle pieces don't fit.

Extricate yourself before you can be discontinued.
All pretense suspended.

Master Plan

Congratulating herself
On winning the lottery

She smacks herself
On the head

And heads
Home to hide

Her ticket
In a shoebox

Under the bed

Spelling It Out

Pay attention to the moon—
There's a secret code
in the order of phases.
There's a code of honor
in the constellations,
order in the alignment
of days and decisions,
seconds and syllables.
It's all stirred up
in the spelling.

In the Cards

It's a magic trick
but nobody knows it—

A sleight of hand
for the hand that bites you.

There's a magician
at the table of confusion

dealing the cards
and setting the rhythm,

sending out smoke and rust
in handwritten letters

transmitted by tea leaves
for reading and believing.

Change of Plans

Don't waste your time—
The poster child for change is knocking
down your door, kicking away reservations
like a spray of shooting stars certain
in their stream of reasons.

Why refuse to recognize the smears
of your visions? Opt out of second
chances? One domino determines
the doubts of another and any other time
you could count the days

like trophies on a bed of posies.
You could change your mind—
Outgrow yourself and reconsider
the options, limber and liable,
like Plan B.

Wild Onions

I don't mind—
you have the right look
of someone under a spell

The mystique
of an imaginary captive
with no hope of being reunited

with wild cousins
and wishful thinking.
I find

you cannot
learn from the weeds
without returning.

Written in the Stars

The world offers a multitude of selves
in a shoebox of causes and threats,
regrets and options.

There's no straight line to uncertainty,
no recipe for rewindings,
no gilded words from guardian angels.

You can't look back but you can memorize
the names of stars and spin the sentences—
and try to conjure an epiphany.

www.ingramcontent.com/pod-product-compliance
Lightning Source LLC
LaVergne TN
LVHW090117080426
835507LV00040B/1059